armorless

armorless

poems by

Carol Lipszyc

Cover design by Shay Culligan
Cover image by Nikhil N. on Unsplash
Author photo by Michael Carrino

ISBN: 978-1-63980-960-8

Kelsay Books
502 South 1040 East, A-119
American Fork, Utah 84003
Kelsaybooks.com

Acknowledgments

Thank you to the following publications and websites, in which versions of these poems previously appeared:

The Dalhousie Review: "Agnostic Standing Before Trinity Anglican Church (Old Thornhill)"

The Jewish Literary Journal: "Sabbath Prayer"

Lothlorien Poetry Journal: "The Gymnasts," "Munro," "Prayer for the Undeserving," "Turning Points"

Poetica Review: "Boy on Stoop," "Trombone Man"

The Quarantine Review TQR: "armourless"

YourPoemaDay YouTube channel, read by David Vickery www.youtube.com/watch?v=sxbGNBOAT5Y: "armorless"

Contents

Agnostic Standing Before Holy Trinity Anglican Church (Old Thornhill)

Church bells chime on Brooke Street,
their music box melody
cradled in the lap of a noonday sun.

I stand before a foreign house of prayer,
its frame a robe of old white linen,
its steeple crowned by a weathervane of brass gold.

Cool cap of air rustles the leaves of waking trees.
A neighbor clears his front yard of winter's neglect,
no admission of sin in the underbrush.

Where is the well-worn hymn to spring? The isolate earth
waits only for a seedling place, ample and protected,
and a kneeling shadow whose hands till beauty.

The Signaling Tree

The moment passes. The moment endures.
On the edge of a sparse lawn, at the corner
of a street marked: *no exit,*

a maple leaf tree reveals her rust-colored petticoat,
the fiery swoop and tassel of her skirt.
On her crown, laid bare, silver metallic
branches signal the pending cold.

How intimate and defiant her surrender,
yielding to winter's mandate of neutral white
in a paroxysm of color.

House of Sparrows

Is it a house divided—
this mesh wire miniature globe
and its pink cymbal roof?
Or a resting nest whose occupants
sing in staccato tempo?

Along the edge of Lake Champlain
and the mindful watch of an oak tree,
a pair of sparrows perched on a wire
dart in and out of their love cage,
rocking gently in a neighbor's garden.

How they flash in the air with heart flutter strokes
a tremble of wings that we name—
trepidation—their heads bobbing
to make constant
the whirring field.

Of All Things—A Rust Bucket

Danny Masks, *Bucket* (photo)

Rust bucket glazed in an alchemy of gold.
Timelines like tree rings
worn by the regimen of chores.

From out of a woodchip toolshed,
past the untilled corner of a fenced-in-yard,
he trails grasses turned brittle,
hand-held metal clanging at his side.

Within her small sphere—a buoyancy
in the carrying and emptying,
filling and refilling
of water, seed, and refuse.

She is a wellspring of modest means:
salve in the quenching of fire,
vessel in the capturing of rain,
prop in the nursery's book of rhyme
when climbing hills on cue.

We say to die is to kick the bucket,
assigning her the gravest role of timekeeper.

Yet here no more than a verse in tow,
brief and stolid in praise
for a simple, cylindrical deliverer
of practical things.

The Gymnasts

Richard Kalvar, *Somersaults in Long Island* (photo)

Three children on a playing field
navigate their independence.

Center back, near the chain link fence,
a girl in summer shorts leaves an imprint in mid-air,
her legs extending to an acute-angled V of inequality,
her limber body on a slant, hands unevenly planted on the grass
in a stance of untapped determination.

To the left, a boy lands flat on his back and buttocks.
His legs have not yet capitulated: he is holding them up in the air,
knees bent, the soles of his feet bleached white,
as he rebuilds his stability.

To the right, near the edge of the frame, the smallest of the flock
lies on her side, her legs apart, her hands hallowing the grass.
She is resting after her tumble, the ribbon on her print dress,
strings on a parachute.

Indelible moment when children test pilot their bodies
on flights of their own making.

In the Days of Corona

seven in the morning and the walls turn blood orange
mother of geometry   fruit peeled of its skin
the sun has morphed into a circle of mandarin red
bobbing in the sky and I imagine I have looked up
from a laboring field of van Gogh's

this in the time of silent streets and acrid fear in the hallways
when our grasp of the future is vapor in the night air
and the sun is a viral fire that brandishes
beauty and terror in one collective breath

armorless

The diagnosis is set in blood—a deficiency
bearing the name of the supermarket chain IgA.

Rooted in syllables so steady,
the term falsely calms the ear:
i-mmu-no-glo-bu-lin-A.

My flimsy mask penetrable
against the red-hot spike-headed Corona,
I renounce every fingerprint,
wipe the counter clean of contaminants,

dream of molecules shaped in the ordained letter Y,
their binding limbs, a balance of heavy and light chains,

while antibodies charge against foreigners,
spilling in from a land called *Pathogenia.*

Is there a Ninja warrior who neutralizes her enemy—
a foe that can breach the bolt of cells,
penetrate the frail bone, the fragile root?

I am ready to learn her language, assume her alias,
don a crimson mask, sheath of iron,
catapult through portent air.

Kunoichi, I will call you in your native tongue.
Kunoichi, the days of a heroine may be slim in number,
but how they surge through the blood
in signature speed and bold color.

Sabbath Prayer

Maze of yellow tape around the jungle gym.
Color wheel of red swing slides and green monkey bars
abandoned.

Absent too jockeying limbs, mother hens pedaling
soft alarm, the high-pitch tag and see-saw
of children's voices.

In their stead, from a balcony high,
a plaintive morning prayer, *Shachrit,*
her Dorian threads of melody blessing the resting hours.

I look to the lone worshipper facing Jerusalem,
his blue and white *tallit* draped overhead.

Feet away at the rim of the park,
an April wind whips the maple-leaf emblem of Canada,
her flagpole clanging in unforgiving meter.

Zoom Blues

Faces loom on a grid panel
of liquid crystal and split glass.

Cast of advocates, naysayers, and negotiators
pop up in talking boxes—modern day mock-up of
old Hollywood Squares.

Behind the scenes, coded algorithms keep time,
spew facts, spin and wring them dry.

Dazed by the roll call of calamity,
a torpedo of crises,
we pull away from the camera,
rear view mirror reflecting back the years
we neglected to count.

Retiree

shunning the elevator
where the cutting breath
of the marauder lurks

she clambers down
a steep grey staircase
past desolate walls
that rotate in their likeness

floor numbers painted in pumpkin orange
thick arrows pointing the way

yet across a fanciful arc of time
wide enough to mark her passage

she counts down in breathless descent
like the pent-up schoolgirl she once was

counts forward on her return
like the woman of advancing years she has become

chips running low in the rows
of her memory bank

Forgetfulness

Words they tumble
into memory's lost bin
Though age can enlighten
what the years rescind.

My train of thought
stops dead on the track
I switch the order
of phrases I hatch.

It's a kind of attrition
a receding line
When sequence vanishes
in a fraction of time.

Did I just take that pill?
where, oh, where are my keys?
Will somebody call
my cell phone, please?

Calendared dates
omitted, unsaved
Quotidien things
misplaced, mislaid.

A shorter version
remains of my story
A fleeting reserve
in my inventory.

Welcome forgetfulness
sporadic and plain
You're part of my profile
my new middle name.

i

can the small "i" suffice?
no capital letters to trumpet my aloneness
nothing but a demure vertical line topped with a dot
to capture miniature me
brittle sometimes buoyant bellicose me

Woolf claimed all i needed was a
room of my own   well
i have long satisfied that condition
and wish i had the means to
embrace possibility again

to succumb once more to the lure
of light in the world

Trombone Man

Lee Friedlander, *Mr. and Mrs. Eddie Morris, New Orleans, 1958* (photo)

Mr. Morris, how firmly you press your lips
to sound the polished bell.

Cramped quarters, furniture stacked high,
your wife stands at the wings, parting a floral lace curtain,
sealing an oath between you.
At the forefront, you face the camera,
skin lined and swelled with wear.

Unflinching eyes,
you hold your trombone easily, assuredly.

Sheen of silk satin on your jacket lapel,
you slide the trombone with your fingers, your thumb—
here wider, there narrowing in—
the have and have-nots of a lifetime.

More than the sturdy, sure-footed papa, trombone man,
you rollick and roll in the tailgate style of Kid Ory,
filling pockets of rhythm as piano and horn sing,
soaring over narrow corridors of black and white,
as you pose for posterity.

Conjuring a Song

Melody weaves through the air—
a thrush cooing on branches.
I lean in to listen,
pluck at strings, press on keys
like a rambunctious child
testing gravity and harmony.
And if the lines please,
as the stems of notes spin before me,
I sing back by heart.

Deck of words shuffle in my hands,
break in half, fall in sequence,
disclosing their meaning.
I give voice to the crisp cut of consonants,
succumb to the allure of vowels,
recite the story in song.

The marriage of words and music
is a marriage of necessity and inspiration,
a fusion of elements I cannot name
but aim to conjure
in the lighting of a star.

A Poet Attempts to Define Intuition

Band of neurons. Spiral line of light.

In a remote Tucson gallery,
my eyes fix on a photograph by Wright Morris:
split wood chair in a bare-boned room,
palette of silver grey,
spindles cast in oblique shadow,
the call of absent voices.

I could enter a home space on the Great Plains,
her acres tilled and sowed some hundred years ago
and reinvent within her small frame
a new storied rhythm in the
guise of a poem.

Quartet on the Theme of Reading and Writing

To embark upon a book
adjust to mood and tenor
Orientate your sight
when first that world you enter.

Structure in composition
is essential to praxis
Like ball-and-socket joints
moving bones along the axes.

If you rail against the system
in a prose diatribe
You will lose the very reader
you had hoped to subscribe.

Read aloud read with care
and the work itself will answer
Once the poem or the narrative
becomes the new master.

What I Have Learned from Fairy Tales

The stepmother Queen
is callous and hollow
A villain whose lead
her subjects will follow.

Beauty is coveted
accolades sought
With a magical mirror
her vanity prop.

Few are the options
at a girl's disposal
The fairest impel
a marriage proposal.

A company of seamstresses
collaborative mice
Fashion a ballgown
bound to entice.

Slippers of glass
for dainty soles
A spell that breaks
when midnight tolls.

Who comes to the rescue?
whose image is true?
We fasten our hearts
to the myth that ensues.

Let us whirr and spin
draw spools of thread
Turn straw to gold
Prince Charming wed.

But curb curiosity
stay close to the path
As the predator waits
for girls in red caps.

Be wary of wolves
in smooth coats of fur
Who con the naïve
in voices that lure.

The prick of a finger
sheds blood on the snow
Build sturdy your house
lest a high wind blow.

And on this end note
I close the chapter
Of my fairy tale moral
for the here and after.

Long-suffering females
will channel rebirth
They water the twigs
and nurture the Earth.

Munro (Fiction Coming to Life, or
A Life Mirrored in Fiction)

I

Family secrets—
a nest of wild bird eggs
buried and abandoned
under matted straw.

Incriminations, denials
crack the back porch wall
of a daughter's summer vacation

shatter the length width
and bone of her womanhood

the scent of her stepfather
sealing the close violated air
of her bedroom.

　　　　II
Silence deepens
as the printed pages roll.
Auteur, luminary with the sharpest eye
and a bloodhound's nose
for revealing human frailty.

III
Beloved among literary icons
Munro's trophy is set on a marble base
and truth withheld in a mass media cover

till a spade breaks the still grass plot
its blade plunging through the tangle of roots
the sanctity of motherhood

to muddy, deface
the sublimely crafted anatomy
of story.

Boy on Stoop

Helen Levitt, 1940 (photo)

Boy on cement stoop leans against bricks
of charcoal grey and mud brown:

elbow perched on knee,
profile caught in a flash of white,
shadow of dirt on the nape of his neck,

sullen resignation in the narrow reach of his eye,
the dipped line of his jaw,
his monochrome mouth.

Over the clamor of tenement walls,
this son of the working poor
will soon outgrow his britches,
brace against the chasm
that looms across a remote sky.

For the moment, huddled in the nook
of a street unnamed (shot in a quizzical slant),
he may empty the pockets
of his oversize jacket,

cull what remains in the cupped
palm of his hands.

Prayer for the Undeserving

Sing a hymn for the troubled world
for tyrannies that rage and rampage
under the banner of their *brand* of God.

Each claiming prime share of the heavens—
a single shining truth.

Each with its army of believers,
followers, stragglers,
their devoted and dismayed.

Some who adhere too closely to the word,
their very breath fraying the sacred page.
Some who malign the word
till it turns dark and disfigured.
Some who scan for the gist of the word,
claiming hard-earned wisdom of its meaning.
Some who dispense with the word
like lint off their shoulders.

A cornucopia of voices—
its pitch ever rising
without a center upon which to rest
and build.

A tower of misanthropes—
the biblical rabble from whom
we all descend.

Hymn to the Letter H

The letter h carries within its boundaries
a multitude of possibilities
for poets, sages, and demons alike.

Forlorn letter, the letter h—
contrarian.

Sometimes it is the silent witness
to the cutting block of time
hour by hour by hour.

Sometimes it aspires to the ideal
strung up in the sky by cotton-soft clouds
that evaporate before our eyes,
and in its polar half
descends into shrapnel—

heaven and hell and the earth between
which we inhabit.

There is the brick-and-mortar *house*
with its utilitarian design,
and in love there is found the *home* of kinship.

There is a more guttural h to name
phantom fighters in airless tunnels,
zealots that burn seas:

Hamas, Hezbollah and the Houthis.
Alliteration numbs the ear,
their rocket missiles fueled by long-festering
hate.

A list of verbs that begins with h is unsolicitous:
to *harass, harangue, heckle,*
to *hamper* and *harm.*

And alongside that which strips away—calcifies—
there is the omnipresent *humor, hope, health*
which we offer up gratis on dollar-store cards
till the words hang loosely on limb and body

all the while gathering tinder to fire
for the centrifugal force at bay:
our beleaguered and robust *hearts.*

The Simmering Earth

in the haze of the sun, a mist of steam
floats over the green manicured grass

phantom band of infrared light
traps the midday heat on field and gravel

thwarting the cooling hour

Reversals

The very young and old
shuffle as they coordinate
their primacy of space.

When a flash of lightning strikes
I dread the boom of thunder—
a fearful aging child forever tricked by the speed
of light.

Turning Points

Ignite the ordinary
and the flicker of a flame
can fan a bonfire
in the imaginative chain.

Hone in on the dusk
as the shutters half-close
When the rim of the dawn's
coral light is exposed.

The River Tells Us So

song lyric to accompany Dave Grusin's *River Song*

It's the flow and the pull and the winding of the water
The bend of its path and the curving of its spine
The stream at our feet and the bank that we will follow
The valley so steep and the rock along the line

It's the ribbon of life a miracle in motion
And it carries the word through the moving hands of time

And he came and he rose and he gathered all our sorrow
And we wade in his grace and the river tells us so

It's the sand and the seed and the bed where fishes slumber
It's the mouth of the river that opens to the sea
If we care if we look if we heed if we but wonder
At the secrets it holds
Then the river sets us free
If we care if we look if we heed if we but listen
To the secrets it holds
Then the river tells us so

And he came and he rose and he gathered all our sorrow
And we wade in his grace and the river tells us so

Over the ages pages immemorial
The river bathed and sustained and
Restored us one and all
Gift of mother earth
The ebb and flow of good
Rising higher now than we could ever rise

Keep us safe on course
Though wind-filled rain may blind
In my faith I find the strength to carry on
Like the river runs
Forever more through mountains to its home

About the Author

A retired associate professor of English and teacher education in the SUNY system, Carol Lipszyc has published three books of poetry: a chapbook, *In the Absence of Sons* (Kelsay Books, 2020); an anthology on the heart, *The Heart is Improvisational* (Guernica, 2017), which she both edited and contributed to; and her lyrical poetry collection, *Singing Me Home* (Inanna, 2010). Her book of short stories on children and adolescents in the Holocaust, *The Saviour Shoes and Other Stories* (2014), was published by Inanna.

www.ingramcontent.com/pod-product-compliance
Lightning Source LLC
Chambersburg PA
CBHW030815090426
42737CB00010B/1283